Table of Contents

INTRODUCTION

There was a time when a woman spent hours monograming bed and table linens for her trousseau. Sadly, this tradition seems to have faded in recent times and we find ourselves treasuring what pieces remain from our grandmother's day. This book was inspired by the desire to keep a sense of this tradition alive but with a new twist. Working, as I do, with the delicate laces and fabrics used in Heirloom Sewing, it seems quite natural to shape lace into monograms. Many of these laces are made in the same patterns as the antique laces, so we have that link with the past.

The revival of silk ribbon embroidery, with it's sensuous texture and association with luxury, allows us to add further personal touches. A simple stitch can come alive in silk ribbon as with no other fibre. What better way to compliment a monogram than with a birth month flower? Be true to life when creating your embroidery or, let your imagination go. There is sure to be a colour in silk ribbon that will please you.

Women tend to form emotional bonds that endure over the years. Only another woman would appreciate the time and tender sentiments stitched into a gift. Although I have presented the monograms and flowers on pillows, do not let this restrict you. You may wish to mark a birthday, a christening, a wedding or just a friendship. What better way than to tuck a few flowers amongst some lace and a froth of ruffles?

SUPPLIES AND NOTIONS

FABRICS

A variety of fabrics have been used for the samples photographed for this book, from the silk of store bought pillows, to the fine fabrics used for heirloom sewing. The monograms are easiest to work on sheer or semi-sheer fabrics such as silk organdy (which is not as abrasive as cotton organdy) or Swiss batiste. The flowers could be stitched on any fabric that does not damage the ribbon.

When an embroidery hoop is inconvenient, the use of polyester fleece (the type used for quilted placemats) is very helpful to support the fabric while you stitch. You will need enough to cover your pillow top.

LACE

French Valencienne and English insertion laces work best. These beautiful cotton laces have gathering threads woven into the heading (straight edges), which allow you to shape them easily. Narrow insertions of 6mm (1/4") to 1cm (3/8") work best for the alphabet given. For an antique look, these laces can be dyed with tea or coffee.

SILK RIBBON

Only silk is silk! It comes in a wonderful pallet of colours and your flowers will have a luminous, lifelike quality. 4mm and 7mm widths of silk ribbon have been used to create Birth Month Flowers. The colour numbers have been listed for your guidance only. Be brave and choose to stitch in colours of your liking.

OTHER FIBRES

100% cotton fine sewing thread (60/2 weight) to match the lace will make the stitching of your monograms more delicate. Embroidery floss and gold metallic machine sewing thread were used to complete the flowers.

NEEDLES AND PINS

Use a fresh (fine) #60 or #70 machine needle for stitching your monograms by machine. For those who prefer hand sewing, pin stitch the lace monograms with a #26 tapestry needle.

Good quality silk pins work best with fine laces and fabrics.

A good selection of hand sewing needles will make your embroidery go faster and easier. Invest in a package of #22 chenille (for 4mm silk ribbon) and #20 or #18 chenille (for 7mm silk ribbon) so you can have several colours threaded up at one time. For embroidery floss and metallic thread, try #6 or #8 milliner needles. They pass through fabric and ribbon without leaving a big hole. They also make wonderfully easy French Knots. For a laying tool, try a large darning needle or wool needle.

Needlework tweezers make shaping the lace much easier.

WORKING SURFACE

A piece of foamboard about 40cm (15") square makes an excellent portable pinning surface. It comes in white (so you can see your pattern through the fabric) and is available in large sheets at office and art supply stores. You will find it useful for many needlework projects besides shaping lace.

STITCHING YOUR MONOGRAM

Make a plan or sketch of your project to help you with placement. Trace your monogram onto a sheet of paper to make it easier to handle. Secure your fabric over monogram pattern to your working surface with pins in at least the four corners to prevent shifting while you work.

Pin your lace to the fabric, beginning at the tail end of the letter. Pin and shape one section of the monogram at a time, being careful not to stretch the lace. "Stick" pin on the outside edge of the curves. With your needlework tweezers or a pin, pull up the outside thread of the lace heading ("selvedge") to allow the lace to gather and lay flat. Distribute the gathers evenly. Remove the "stick" pins and replace them with "flat" pins as each section is shaped. (See photo on Pattern Page.) Lace may protrude from the folds made to form the points of the letters. Do not worry as this lace will be trimmed away after stitching. When all pinning is finished, hand baste both edges of the lace insertion. Remove pins.

Now you can machine stitch. Use a narrow zigzag stitch, approximately 1 1/2 width, length 3/4. Adjust your setting so stitching just covers the width of the lace's heading. If you prefer hand work, pin stitch the lace in place.

TIP: You may use water soluble marker to draw the tapered ends of the letters as a guide for your stitching. (Take care to use nothing that can not be removed easily.) Be sure to dip the whole piece of fabric in cool water to remove all the marker after stitching.

Trim all threads and lace ends. Press.

If you choose to use polyester fleece to support your fabric for embroidery, cut a piece the same size as your fabric and baste the edges together. From this point on, treat the two as one. Now you are ready to add flowers to your monogram.

GENERAL INSTRUCTIONS FOR EMBROIDERY WITH SILK RIBBON

Cut a piece of silk ribbon approximately 30cm (12") long. (Keeping the length short prevents the ribbon from wearing while stitching.)

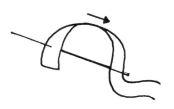

To thread your needle, pass the ribbon through the eye of the needle. Pull enough through to be able to pierce the ribbon 2cm (3/4") from the end. Pull from the other end to lock the ribbon on the needle.

When all your stitching is finished, whip all the tails to the back of your embroidery with fine sewing thread. Not only does this ensure your work will not pull out, but prevents "shadows" of ends showing through on the right side of your work.

You may choose to stitch the flower first and then the leaves and stems, or to work in the reverse order. Only when the flowers lay over the leaves must you stitch the background first. Otherwise, there is no right or wrong order.

Refer to the Stitch Glossary on pages 30 / 31 for silk ribbon embroidery stitch techniques.

JANUARY

Carnation

Carnation - Fickleness, woman's love

Carnations come in an abundance of colours so take your choice.
You can stitch petals of the flowers in either 7mm or 4mm ribbon.
7mm will give you a larger flower.

Lightly draw a tiny oval as a base
approximately 5cm (3/16") for
ruching.

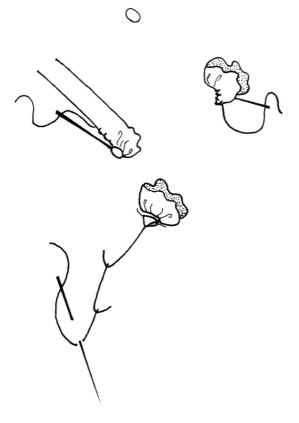
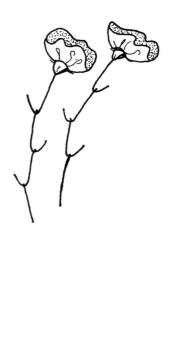

Petals - 7mm red #2 - *Ruched ribbon.*
Calyx - 4mm green #31 - *Loop stitch,* couched.
Stem - Floss to match #31, two strands - *Feather stitch.*

JANUARY

FEBRUARY

MARCH

JANUARY

Snowdrop

Snowdrop - Good omen, Hope

Snowdrops tend to push their way through the snow
to herald the coming of Spring, hence their meaning.

When working the couched stems, try threading up two milliners'
needles, one to be used to lay the stem, the other used to couch
the stem in place.

Stitch Order

couching stitch

Petals - 4mm white #3 - *Straight stitch.*
Calyx - 4mm green #31 - *Straight stitch.*
Leaves - 4mm green #31 - *Ribbon stitch.*
Stems - Floss to match leaves, two strands, couched.

FEBRUARY

Violets (Viola)

Violets - Modesty

Napolean loved them so much, he always gave Josephine a bouquet of violets on their wedding anniversary. Violets have been used in medicines since the time of the Greeks.

Violets come in many shades of pink and mauve.

 Stitch Order

 Couch the Loop stitch
and the stem.

Petal - 4mm mauve #102 - *Straight stitch.*
Bud - 4mm mauve #102 - *Loop stitch.*
Leaves - 4mm green #72 - *Ribbon stitch.*
Stems - Floss to match leaves, two strands, couched.
Centres - Floss, gold, two strands, *French Knot.*

FEBRUARY

Primrose (Primula)

Primrose - Good luck, Youth

From the Latin meaning first, Primroses come in many colours.
In Victorian times, they were a favourite garden flower.

Stitch Order

Flowers - 4mm yellow #15 - *Ribbon stitch.*
Buds - 4mm yellow #15 - *Straight stitch.*
Leaves - 4mm green #72 - *Ribbon stitch.*
Stems - Floss to match leaves, two strands, *Straight stitch.*
Centres - Floss a tone darker than petals, two strands, *French Knot.*

MARCH

Daffodil

Daffodil - Affection, Chivalry

A member of the large Narcissus family, this one is the familiar
long trumpeted daffodil.

Halo - Note length of stitches and stitch order.

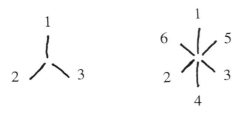 

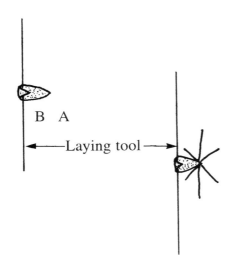

Halo petals - 4mm yellow #12 - *Straight stitch.*
Trumpet - 4mm yellow #15 - blunt *Ribbon stitch.*
Leaves - 4mm green #72 - *Straight stitch*, couched, twisted.
Stems - Floss to match leaves, two strands, *Straight stitch.*

MARCH

Jonquil

Jonquil - Regard

A member of the Narcissus family.

Halo  Stitch Order

Trumpet - Ruched ribbon - gather just
enough to get ribbon
to stand up.

Halo - 4mm yellow #12 - *Straight stitch.*
Trumpet - 4mm yellow #12 - *Ruched ribbon*, gathered just
enough to make the trumpet stand up.
Leaves - 4mm green #72 - *Straight stitch*, couched and twisted.
Stems - Floss to match leaves, two strands, couched.
Centres - Floss, gold, two stands, *French Knot.*

APRIL

Sweet Pea

Sweet Pea - False modesty, Departure

This climbing plant is a member of the Pea family
and comes in many colours.

Flower
large ruffle centre - 2 Ribbon stitches

medium ruffle

small ruffle

Ruffle - 7mm pink #7 - *Ruched ribbon.*
Centres - 4mm pink #68 - *Ribbon stitch.*
Sepals - 4mm green #32 - *Ribbon stitch.*
Leaves - 4mm green #32 - *Ribbon stitch.*
Stems and tendrils - Floss to match leaves, two strands, couched.

APRIL

Daisy

Daisy - Simplicity, Beauty

A member of the large Chrysanthemum family, the Shasta Daisy
is stitched here. It comes in white only.

   Stitch Order

Note different lengths of petals
to get perspective.

   Bud - 2 Straight stitches
Calyx - couched Loop stitch

Petals - 4mm white #3 - *Straight stitch.*
Centre - 4mm yellow #15 - *Straight stitch*, padded
(Make a small *French knot* in the centre of the flower and
cover with a *Straight stitch* to get a slightly raised effect).
Calyx - 4mm green #72 - *Loop stitch*, couched.
Leaves - 4mm green #72 - *Straight stitch*, couched and twisted.
Stems - Floss to match leaves, two strands, couched.

MAY

Lily - of - the - Valley

Lily - of - the - Valley - Return of happiness

A favourite of brides, it was once an ingredient of love potions.

Flowers

Leaves - Pull up a bit more ribbon to the surface on one side than the other.

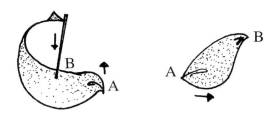

Put needle through ribbon to one side rather than the middle.

Stems - Floss to match leaves, two strands, *Stem stitch.*
Flowers - 4mm white #3 - *Loop stitch.*
Start at base of stem, work flowers towards end,
gradually making the loops smaller.
Leaves - 7mm green #32 - *Ribbon stitch.*

APRIL

MAY

JUNE

MAY

Hawthorn

Hawthorn - Hope

The hawthorn tree, with its characteristic sharp thorns, is a member of the Rose Family. In the spring it can be found in country hedgerows, covered in pink or white blossoms. In the fall it bears bright red berries.

Flower 5 petals

Leaves 2 small Ribbon stitches

add 1 long stitch overlapping from the same base point

Stem   Fly stitch

Bud   Loop stitch, couched

Flowers - 4mm white #3 - *Ribbon stitch.*
Buds - 4mm white #3 - *Loop stitch* couched with green.
Leaves - 4mm green #72 - *Ribbon stitch.*
Stem - Floss to match leaves, two strands, *Straight stitches.*
Branch - 4mm brown #37 - *Straight stitch*, twisted.
Stamens - Floss one strand each of red and gold, *Detached Pistol stitch.*

JUNE

Rose

Rose - Love

In Victorian days, the colour of the rose had special meaning.
Friends and lovers often used roses to send messages to one another.

5 arm star in floss.

French knot of ribbon in centre.

Weave ribbon over and under arms.

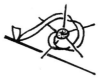

Lazy Daisy surrounds French knot.

Flowers:

Red rose - 4mm dk red #49 - *French knot* in the centre to support woven rose
4mm medium red #2 - Woven rose.

Pink rose - 4mm dk red #49 - *French knot* in the centre to support woven rose
4mm medium red #2 - Woven rose
4mm - dk pink #25 - Woven rose.

Buds - 4mm dk pink #25 - *French knot*
4mm pink #24 - *Lazy daisy.*
Leaves - 4mm green #171 - *Ribbon stitch.*
Stems - Floss to match leaves, two strands, *Stem stitch.*

Preparing Your Monogram

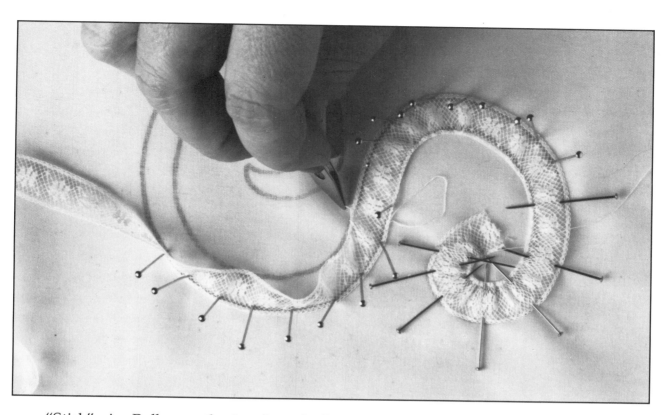

"Stick" pin. Pull up gathering threads. Distribute fullness evenly, then "flat" pin.

E F

G H

JUNE

Honeysuckle

Honeysuckle - Ties of love, Rustic

Not as familiar but easier to stitch, this variety is the Siberian Honeysuckle which bears fragrant pink flowers.

Large leaves are broad Lazy Daisy stitches.

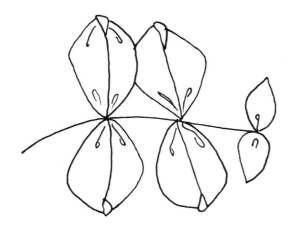
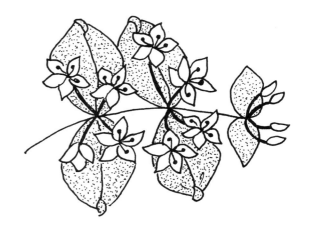

Flowers - 4mm pink #68 - *Straight stitch.*
Buds - 4mm pink #68 - *Straight stitch.*
Leaves - 7mm green #20 - *Lazy daisy* for large, *Straight stitch* for small.
Branch - Floss, brown, two strands, *Stem stitch.*
Floral stems - Floss, pale green, two strands, *Straight stitch.*
Stamens - Floss, pale yellow, two strands, *Detached pistol stitch.*

Tip: Stitch the branch and leaves first.

JULY

Larkspur

Larkspur - Lightheartedness, Brightness

The larkspur is a variety of Delphinium. The Greeks named them Delphinion as they thought, when tossed by the wind, these flowers looked like dolphins at play. Larkspur comes in many colours with bright green foliage.

Stitch Order

2

3

1 - "Dolphin" tail on large flowers

6

4

5

Flowers and Buds - 4mm blue #117 - *Straight stitch.*
Stem - Floss, bright green, two strands - *Stem stitch.*
Leaves - Floss, bright green, two strands - *Sheaf stitch.*
Centres - Floss, pale yellow, two strands - *French knot.*

JULY

AUGUST

SEPTEMBER

JULY

Water Lily

Water Lily - Invocation

A beautiful water plant with delicately coloured flowers.

Stitch Order

First layer

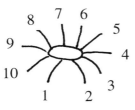

Second layer

Third layer

Ruched lily pad - couched with 3 - 4 long stitches

Flower - 4mm pink #7 - *Straight stitch.*
Leaves - 7mm green #31 - *Ruched ribbon* couched with matching floss, 2 strands.

Tip: Stitch the leaves first so the flowers can overlap them.

AUGUST

Gladiolus

Gladiolus - Success

These spectacular flowers come in so many colours that they are
registered by number. So let your imagination run wild!

Stitch Order

First layer

Second layer

Flowers - 7mm red #2 - *Ribbon stitch.*

Buds - 7mm red #2 - *Straight stitch.*

Lower stem - 4mm green #32 - *Straight stitch.*

Upper stem - Floss, green to match green ribbon, two strands, *Straight stitch*
Fly stitch around the buds.

Centres - Floss, black, two strands, *French knot.*

AUGUST

Poppy

Poppy - Consolation, Heroism

In Europe it was considered beneficial to have poppies growing
in the grain fields. Again, there are many varieties and colours.

Stitch Order

First layer - 2 ruched petals

Second layer - 2 ruched petals

Flower - 4mm apricot #169 - *Ruched ribbon* 4 petals.
Bud - 4mm green #31 - *French knot.*
Bud - Floss, green to match bud ribbon, two strands - *Straight stitch.*
Centre - 4mm black #4 - *French knot.*
Stems - Floss, green to match bud, two strands - *Stem stitch.*
Leaves - Floss, green to match bud, two strands - *Feather stitch.*

SEPTEMBER

Aster

Aster - Happiness in old age, Variety

Aster means star, referring to the effect of its petals. It is a member of the composite Chrysanthemum family.

Stitch Order   Vary length of petals

Large Aster

Smaller Aster

Fill centre with French knots

Flower - 4mm blue/mauve #117 - *Straight stitch.*
Leaves - 4mm green #32 - *Straight stitch.*
Centre - Floss, gold, two strands - *French knots.*
Stem - Floss, green to match leaves, couched.

SEPTEMBER

Morning Glory

Morning Glory - Flirtation

A ground cover vine, there are over 200 species in America alone.

Buttonhole stitch

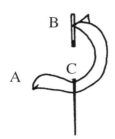

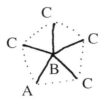

Lightly mark the 5 arms on the fabric.
Come up at A. Stitch from B to C. Repeat
B to C three times. To end, slip under A
and take to back at B.

Leaves

Flowers - 4mm #98 - *Buttonhole stitch*, five stitches in a circle.
Leaves - 4mm green # 32 - *Ribbon stitch*, stitch in pairs
for a heart-shaped leaf effect.
Stems and Tendrils - Floss, green to match leaves, two strands, couched.
Centres - Floss, lemon yellow, two strands - *French knot*.

OCTOBER

Calendula

Calendula - Chagrin

A more familiar name might be Pot Marigold. Shakespeare referred to it as "winking Mary-buds".

Stitch Order

First layer

Second layer

Finish centre with French knot

Flower - 4mm orange #40 - *Straight stitch.*
Centre - 4mm orange #40 - *French knot.*
Leaves - 4mm green #31 - *Straight stitch.*
Stems - 4mm green to match leaves, two strands - *Stem stitch.*

OCTOBER

Cosmos

Cosmos - Duty

A native to Mexico, its lacy foliage made the cosmos a favourite in Grandmother's garden.

Stitch Order

Flower

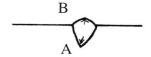 Laying tool holds ribbon flat to 'blunt' end of stitch.

Flowers - 4mm magenta #145 - *Straight stitch.*
Use your laying tool to 'blunt end' the ribbon as you make each petal.
Buds - 4mm magenta #145 - *French knot.*
Buds - Floss, sage green (to match silk ribbon colour #32), two strands -
Straight stitches, one stitch should pierce the bud.
Stems - Floss, sage green, two strands, couched.
Leaves - Floss, sage green, two strands - *Feather stitch.*

NOVEMBER

Chrysanthemum

Chrysanthemum - Longevity, Cheerfulness

In Greek, chrysanthemum means golden flower. A composite family,
there are many varieties, some of which are edible.

Stitch Order

First layer

Second layer - 3 stitches from
between 8 - 7, 7 - 6, 6 - 5.

Leaves 2 small Ribbon stitches

 add 1 long stitch
overlapping from the
same base point

Flowers - 4mm mauve #22 - *Straight stitch.*
Leaves - 4mm green #72 - *Ribbon stitch.*
Stems - Floss, green to match leaves, two strands, couched.

OCTOBER

NOVEMBER

DECEMBER

NOVEMBER

Gardenia

Gardenia - Peace

A beautiful white tropical flower with dark green, waxy leaves.
Its heady scent makes the gardenia a favourite for special occasion corsages.

Flower

Twirl needle and ribbon until ribbon coils.

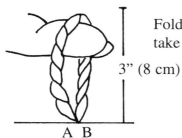 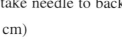

Fold over index finger and take needle to back of work.

3" (8 cm)

A B

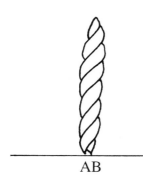

Remove finger. Ribbon will twirl onto itself. If you have ever made cording, this is very similar.

AB

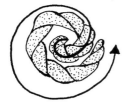

Lay ribbon to form flower. Pin to hold while stitching to fabric. Tuck and tack end of coil.

Flower - 7mm white #3 - *Twirled ribbon,* couched.
Leaves - 7mm green #21 - *Ribbon stitch.*

DECEMBER

Narcissus

Narcissus - Vanity, Egotism

In Greek mythology, Narcissus was a beautiful youth who so loved his own reflection in the water that he was turned into the narcissus flower. Here we have the familiar Paper White Narcissi. The daffodil and jonquil are part of this family.

Stitch Order

Halo

Trumpet - Ruched ribbon - gather just enough to get ribbon to stand up.

Halo - 4mm white #3 - *Straight stitch.*
Trumpet - 4mm yellow #15 - *Ruched ribbon*, gather only enough to make the trumpet stand.
Leaves - 4mm green #20 - *Straight stitch*, twisted and couched.
Stem - Floss, green to match leaves, two strands - *Straight stitch.*
Centres - Floss, bright red, two strands - *Detached pistol stitch.*

DECEMBER

Christmas Rose

Christmas Rose - Pride

Helleborus Niger has been cultivated since Roman times. Its
delicate white and pale pinkish-white flowers are highlighted
by a crown of golden stamens. Known to bloom in snow in winter,
it is a perfect flower to represent December.

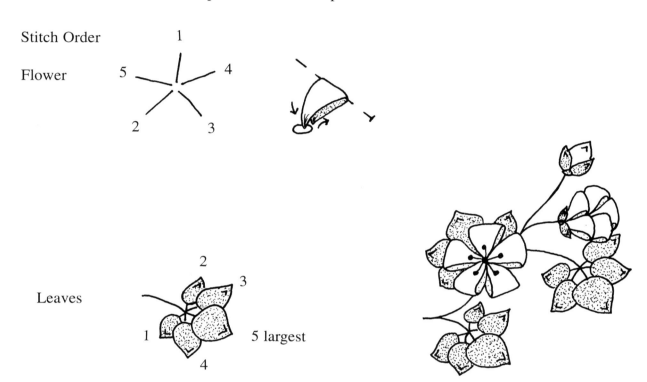

Stitch Order

Flower

Leaves

Flowers - 7mm white #3 - *Loop stitch.*

Buds - 7mm white #3 - *Ribbon stitch.*

Calyx - 4mm green #21 - *Ribbon stitch* and small *Straight stitch*
at the base of the bud.

Leaves - 7mm green #21 - *Ribbon Stitch .*

Stems - Floss, one strand each of dark burgundy and green to
match leaves - *Stem stitch.*

Stamens - Gold metallic thread, double strand - *Pistol stitch* to
couch each of five petals.

Centre - Gold metallic thread, double strand - *French knot(s).*

STITCH GLOSSARY

STRAIGHT STITCH

Twist this stitch or couch it to give more interesting effects.

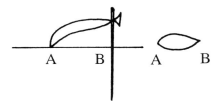

RIBBON STITCH

Needle passes to back through ribbon and fabric.

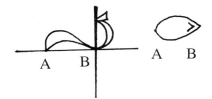

LOOP STITCH

In 7mm for petals (Christmas Rose) or 4mm for Violet buds this stitch is easy to execute. Mark a tiny circle on your fabric for the centre of your flower. Bring your needle to the surface on the outside edge of the circle. Take it to the back on the inside edge of the circle. Use a pin to hold the loop to size as you stitch the next loop. Be careful to pull all your ribbon through from the back with each stitch.

B A

RUCHED RIBBON

This technique can yield so many looks, from lily pads to jonquil trumpets. Do not lock the ribbon on the needle as usual. This time, pull the end of your ribbon to the wrong side (point **A**) to give you a tail about 2.5cm (1"). Grasp opposite sides of the ribbon, one hand above the fabric, the other below. Pull on the bias. With needle and fine sewing thread (knotted), come up at **A**. Take 3 or 4 whip stitches (spaced 1/8" apart) on the short edge of the ribbon. Take the needle to the back at **A**. Ribbon will gather. Repeat this process, spacing the stitches into the fabric, until you have achieved the look you want. When you are almost finished, cut the ribbon so you have just enough to end off. Take the tail to the back as you did at the start, and whip the last little bit into place.

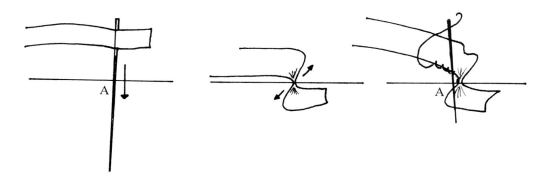

COUCHING

This is simply the technique of taking a stitch with thread or matching floss to hold ribbon or floss in place. These stitches can be so tiny we don't see them (stems) or large so they look like veins (lily pads). Sometimes these stitches allow leaves to bend, giving a more lifelike appearance.

FRENCH KNOT

PISTOL STITCH

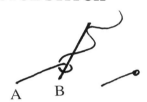

DETACHED PISTOL STITCH

For pistols or stamens that stand free, bring needle and floss to the surface and wrap as for French Knot. Pull the needle through the wrap making a knot on the floss. To control the placement, use the point of the needle to slide the knot down to desired position. Cut floss close to knot.

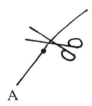

STEM STITCH

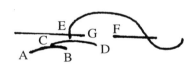

LAZY DAISY

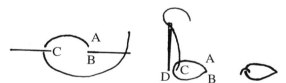

FLY STITCH

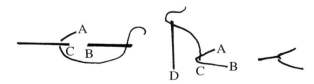

SHEAF STITCH

FEATHER STITCH

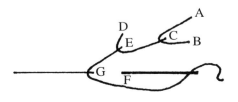

If your favourite sewing or needlework shop does not carry the supplies required in Monograms & Flowers, ask them to contact:

WHOLESALE SUPPLIERS

CANADA

U.S.A.

SILK RIBBON & FINE FABRICS
Trudi Clarkson Sales
Box 28004, North Park Plaza P.O.
Brantford, Ontario N3R 7X5
TEL: (519) 759-4322
FAX: (519) 759-8671

FINE FABRICS
Spechler-Vogel Textiles
234 West 39th Street,
New York, NY 10018
TEL: (800) 223-2031
FAX: (212) 768-4166

LACE & FINE FABRICS
Trudi's Capitol Imports
Box 28004, North Park Plaza P.O.
Brantford, Ontario N3R 7X5
TEL: (519) 759-4322
FAX: (519) 759-8671

LACES & FINE FABRICS
Capitol Imports
P.O. Box 13002
Tallahassee, FL 32317
TEL: (800) 433-5457
FAX: (904) 386-3153

BOOKS, NEEDLES &
NEEDLEWORK TWEEZERS
Grace L. Knott Smocking Supplies Ltd.
86 Larkfield Drive,
Don Mills, Ontario M3B 2H1
TEL: (416) 447-5745
FAX: (416) 447-5413

FINE SEWING THREAD
Mettler Brand   Domcord Belding
                 660 Denison Street,
                 Markham, Ontario L3R 1C1

Zwicky Brand   Husqvarna White
                 1470 Birchmount Road,
                 Scarborough, Ontario M1P 2G1

ACKNOWLEDGEMENTS

Many thanks to Trudi, George, Judy, Peter, Harold, Michelle and, of course, my family without whose help, patience and encouragement this book would not have been done!